The Rainbow Orange

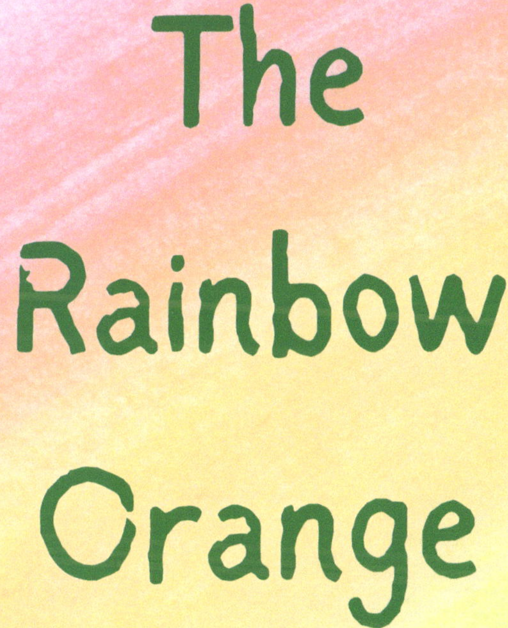

Written and Illustrated by
Lateefat Ibrahim

This is Bale. Bale is a boy.
He is 5 years old.

This is Bale's house. Bale lives here with his mum and dad.

There is a garden in front of the house. Can you see the orange tree in the garden?

There are many oranges in the tree. The oranges are ripe.

Bale is in the garden. Bale is looking at the orange tree. But wait...

Bale sees a rainbow orange in the tree!...

Can you also see the rainbow orange?

Bale can see red, orange and yellow colors.
Do you see more colors?

"Mum!" "Dad!" Shouted Bale. "There's a rainbow orange in our tree!"

Bale's mum and dad rushed into the garden.

They both saw the
rainbow orange too.

"How strange! A rainbow orange!" They chorused.

"I want the rainbow orange, please!" Said Bale. Jumping up and down

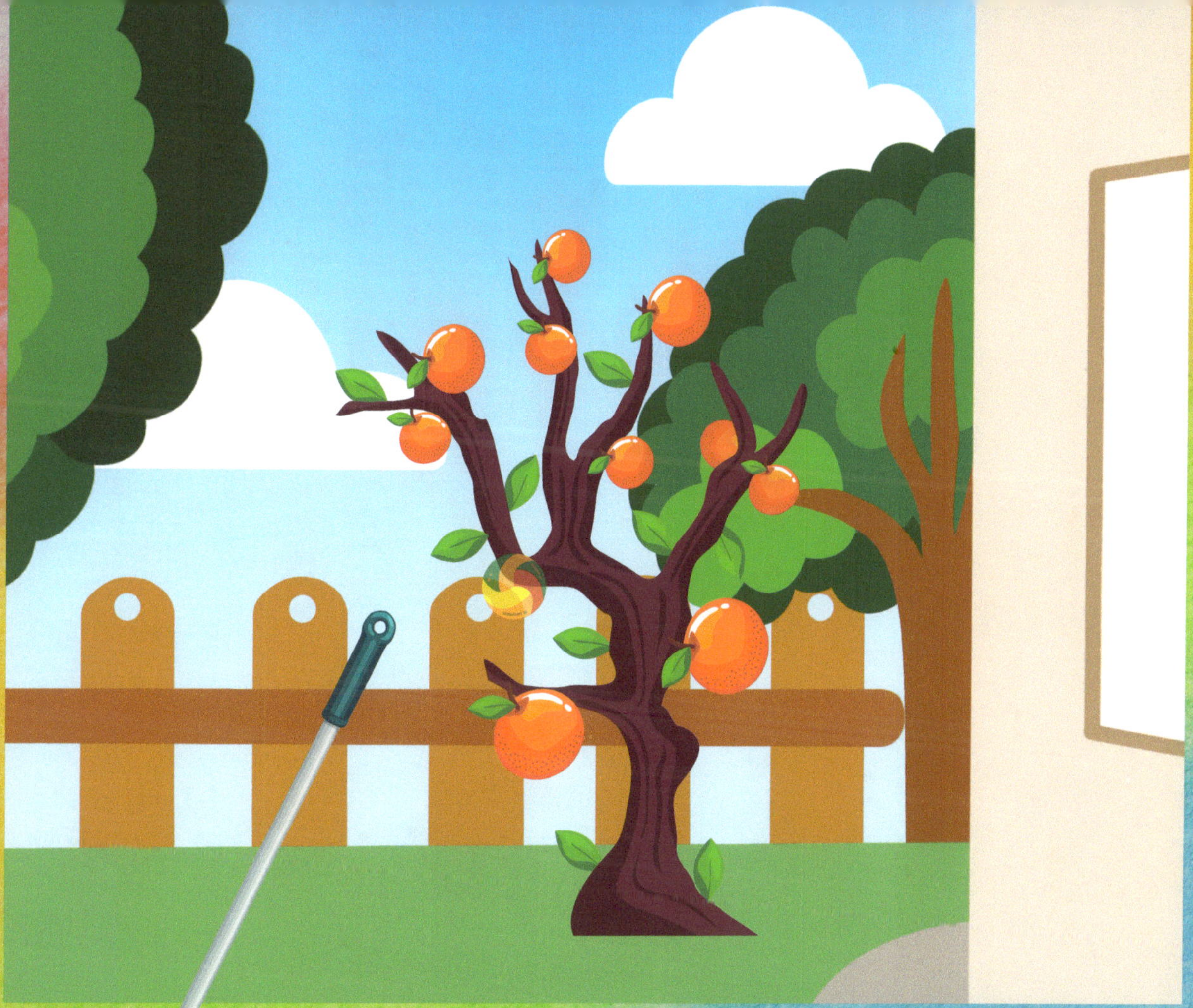

Bale's dad used a mop stick to beat down the rainbow orange.

The rainbow orange floated down...
Bale went to it and lifted it up

He turned it round and round. He saw more colors — green. blue. indigo. and violet.

Can you also see the colors of the rainbow?

"But it's a small ball!" Bale said
Bale was disappointed.
Bale wanted a rainbow orange.

Then he saw Hafsa. his friend. who lives next door running towards him.

"Thank you for finding my rainbow ball!" Said Hafsa.

"It was up in the tree." "I thought it was an orange, a rainbow orange!" Bale told Hafsa.

Bale is now excited. Bale is happy
he found Hafsa's ball.

Hafsa laughed happily.
It was not a rainbow orange
after all. Rather. it is a ball that
is round like an orange.

Everybody laughed at the rainbow
orange that was not quite an orange.